Drag Racing

Jay H. Smith

Reading Consultant:
John Manning, Professor of Reading
University of Minnesota

CAPSTONE BOOKS

an imprint of Capstone Press
Mankato, Minnesota

Capstone Books are published by Capstone Press
151 Good Counsel Drive, P.O. Box 669, Mankato, Minnesota 56002
http://www.capstone-press.com

Library of Congress Cataloging-in-Publication Data
Smith, Jay,
  Drag racing/by Jay Smith.
  p. cm.—(Motorsports)
  Includes bibliographical references and index.
  ISBN 1-56065-230-6
  1. Drag racing—Juvenile literature. [1. Drag racing.] I. Title. II. Series.
GV1029.3.S56 1995
796.7'2—dc21   94-22625
                                                                      CIP
                                                                      AC

Photo Credits
All Sport Photography, cover
Leslie Lovett, 4, 7, 8, 10, 13, 14-15, 16, 18, 21, 22, 24, 26-27, 30, 33,
    34-35, 36, 37, 38, 40

2 3 4 5 6 05 04 03 02 01

Table of Contents

Chapter 1

At a Drag Meet

Since you've never been to a **drag meet** before, you're amazed that there are so many spectators. Fifty thousand fans are packed into the grandstand and along the fences that line the **drag strip**. The first **heat** is about to begin.

You can barely hear all the cheering above the roar of the engines. Some spectators shut their eyes. They want to feel the ground shake as the next pair of **Top Fuel** dragsters **rev** their 5000-**horsepower** engines.

One of the **dragsters** moves into the **burnout area**. Here the driver spins his rear tires in a puddle of water. This cleans the tires for a better grip on the track. The smoke from the burning tires stings your eyes. Or is it **nitro**? This is the kind of fuel the cars use instead of gasoline.

After both cars have had their burnout, the drivers are ready for the start. Amber lights flash. Then the green light is lit and the race begins.

Instead of watching the dragsters, many fans turn their eyes away from the track. The cars are a blur as they roar down the quarter-mile (402.3-meter) strip. In less than five seconds, the race will be over. The cars release the colorful parachutes that help them slow down.

The race is over. It was too close for you to see which dragster crossed the finish line first. Instead, you watch for the results on the electronic scoreboard. When the winner's name appears, the crowd erupts in deafening cheers.

This is the popular and exciting sport of drag racing.

Chapter 2
Drag Racing Today

Dragsters race in many different ways. But all drag races have some things in common.

The Drag Strip

All drag races are a quarter of a mile (.4 kilometer) long. They are run on a drag strip–a paved surface that is straight from start to finish.

Beyond the finish line, there is a **shutdown strip.** This area is where drivers slow down after the race.

On the drag strip there are two lanes for racing. Usually guard rails separate the two lanes. Sometimes only painted lines separate them.

The Top Eliminator

In drag racing, cars race two at a time. The loser is **eliminated**, and the winner moves on to the next round. This continues until only one car remains unbeaten. The winning dragster is called the **top eliminator.**

The Christmas Tree

Drag races are started and timed electronically. Twenty feet (6.1 meters) from the starting line, between the two lanes, is a pole of colored lights called a **Christmas Tree**.

The **pre-stage light** is at the top of the tree. When this small amber light goes on, the drivers move toward the starting line. The **stage light**, also small and amber, is next on the pole. It flashes when the dragsters are on the starting line. There is also a large blue light at the top of the pole. When lit, it means that one of the cars has rolled past the starting line. The driver will have to back up.

The next three lights on the Christmas Tree are the starting lights. These large amber lights flash one after the other every half-second. They tell the drivers to get ready.

The next light on the pole is large and green. When it lights up, it tells the drivers to go. The last light–a red light–goes on only if a driver starts before the green light flashes. Any driver who gets a red light is automatically **disqualified**. There are no second chances in drag racing.

Attacking the Green

Nowhere is driving skill more important in drag racing than at the start of the race. This is where most races are won or lost.

A pair of dragsters blasts out of the starting area as the amber lights turn to green.

A driver needs great reflexes in order to start exactly when the green light goes on. A split second too soon means disqualification. A split second too late can mean defeat.

The very best drivers start at just the right time. This is called "attacking the green."

E.T.

Racing officials record two scores for each dragster. The first is **elapsed time**, or **e.t.** This measures how long it takes the car to complete the race. The car with the lower e.t. wins. The second score measures the dragster's top speed.

Speed Traps

Speed is recorded by two **speed traps**. One is located 66 feet (19.8 meters) from the

starting line. The other is 66 feet (19.8 meters) from the finish line. Electronic beams measure the speed of the cars as they pass by the traps.

Behind the Scenes

Even the best driver cannot win without the best equipment and an excellent **pit-crew**. Drag-racing mechanics are called **wrenches**. Pit-crew leaders are called **chief wrenches**. Some of the top chief wrenches are as famous as the drivers they work for.

Chapter 3
Top Fuelers

Top Fuel cars are the fastest, most expensive, and most dangerous of all dragsters.

Top Fuelers are 25 feet (7.5 meters) long, 3 feet (.9 meter) wide, and 3 feet (.9 meter) high. They weigh almost 2,000 pounds (910 kilograms). Their nicknames–**rails**, **stilettos**, and **slingshots**–are good descriptions of these odd-looking cars.

Breaking the Speed Barriers

In 1988 Eddie Hill became the first Top Fuel driver to finish a race in less than five seconds.

Since then, runs of 4.8 and 4.9 seconds have become very common. In 1992 Kenny Bernstein lowered the mark to 4.794 seconds in his Top Fuel car, *Budweiser King*.

As soon as Eddie Hill had broken the five-second e.t. barrier, all of the top drivers set a new goal. They wanted to be the first to record a top speed of 300 miles (482.8 kilometers) per hour. New technology eventually made it possible. Drivers closed in on the 300-mile (482.8-kilometer) per hour barrier. The fans cheered for their favorites to break the mark.

The Snake

Many fans hoped that Don "The Snake" Prudhomme would be the first to reach 300. In his long career, "The Snake" had won just about every championship. He was one of the three great heroes of the sport, along with Don "Big Daddy" Garlits and Shirley Muldowney, a three-time world champion in the mid-1980s.

Don "The Snake" Prudhomme stands in his driving gear.

Eddie Hill had his supporters, too. Other fans were sure that 1990 Top Fuel points champion Joe Amato would be the one.

Engineering Geniuses

Despite all the championships won by these stars, the two top contenders seemed to be Kenny Bernstein and Gary Ormsby, the 1989 National Hot Rod Association Top Fuel champion. After all, they had the two best drag-racing minds working for them. Lee Beard was Ormsby's team manager. Dale Armstrong was Bernstein's chief wrench. Beard and Armstrong were known as the engineering geniuses of the sport.

An Instant Star

In 1991, **cancer** forced Gary Ormsby to give up his dream. Lee Beard went to work for Pat Austin, a newcomer to Top Fuel racing. Austin had been almost unbeatable in the **amateur** pro-stock class, where he won more than 40 races.

Shirley Muldowney, three-time world champion

A split second too early or too late can mean defeat.
Drag-race drivers need perfect timing.

In March of 1992, Austin became an instant Top Fuel star by setting a new speed record of 295.27 miles (475.2 kilometers) per hour.

301.7 Miles (485.5 Kilometers) Per Hour

This was all the challenge Kenny Bernstein needed. Two weeks later, at the Gatornationals in Gainesville, Florida, he roared down the strip at an amazing speed of 301.7 miles (485.5 kilometers) per hour. To prove it was not just luck, Bernstein broke the 300-mile (482.8-kilometer) per hour barrier two more times that season.

The Million-Dollar Season

A Top Fuel car costs about $150,000. To race one season in top competition can cost another $750,000 to $850,000. Large corporations sponsor all the best drivers.

$1,600 Per Second

Every time a Top Fueler makes a run down the drag strip, it costs as much as $8,000. That's about $1,600 a second. After each run, a Top Fuel engine must be rebuilt. The $7,000 **clutch** is good for only one run. The $3,500 **supercharger** and the $7,000 disc brakes last only one run, too.

There's more. Tires are good for only 20 seconds of racing, or about four runs. Transmissions have to be replaced after 75 seconds. Nitro costs $1,000 for a 50-gallon

(189.3-liter) drum. A Top Fuel car will use
two and a half drums on a typical racing
weekend. The thirsty Top Fuel car needs seven
gallons (26.5 liters) of fuel during the burnout
and another three gallons (11.4 liters) during
the run.

Although expenses are high, top drivers can
win big prize money. The winner of the
Winston World Championship, for example,
receives $150,000.

Blowovers

Drivers know that every run could be their
last. Thanks to strict safety rules and excellent
safety equipment, accidents are rare. But when
accidents do happen, they are very dramatic.
Fans remember them well.

Sometimes Top Fuelers seem to jump like
kangaroos. At very high speeds, the cars can
actually fly off the ground. These **blowovers**
are quite frightening. When the car finally hits
the ground, it may land upside down or
sideways. In any case, the driver is in great
danger.

A Tragic End

Racing fans remember the 1992 Winternationals in Pomona, California. The car of Jimmy Nix left the strip when a part of its front wing broke. The dragster flew over the speed and e.t. traps without breaking the photoelectric beams.

When it landed, the car burst into flames. Somehow Nix survived with only burns on his hands and feet.

Tragically, Jimmie Nix was killed only two years later in a fiery crash at the Motorplex in Ennis, Texas.

Chapter 4

Funny Cars and Pro Stocks

Funny cars and pro stocks are two other popular types of dragsters.

Funny Cars–No Hood, No Doors

At first glance, a funny car looks like a regular car. But if you look again, you see that it's made of one piece. It has no hood or doors. You get in a funny car by lifting the entire body off the frame. This is easy, because the body is made of lightweight fiberglass or plastic, not steel.

Almost as Fast as Top Fuelers

Funny cars have very powerful engines. Their top speed is about 290 miles (466.7 kilometers) per hour. They cover the quarter-mile (.4-kilometer) in 5.1 or 5.2 seconds–almost as fast as Top Fuelers. The leading funny-car drivers are John Force, Dale Pulde, and Jim Epler. Like the world-champion Top Fueler, the funny-car champion can earn $150,000 in prize money.

Pro Stock Cars

Pro stock cars are built like regular cars. They have ordinary dashboards, upholstery, and windows. They may look like the family car, but their engines have been rebuilt and made more powerful. This is why pro stocks are sometimes called "**muscle cars**."

Pro stock cars are not your typical family car. They can run a dragstrip at almost 200 miles (322 kilometers) per hour.

Pro stock cars are slower, safer, and prettier than Top Fuelers and funny cars. Their top speed is about 195 miles (313.8 kilometers) per hour. They run the dragstrip in slightly over seven seconds. Pro stock drivers do not have

to wear protective clothing, but they usually
do, just in case.

The Superstars

Pro stock stars include Jerry Eckman,
Warren "Mr. Horsepower" Johnson, and Rickie
Smith. The winner of the pro stock world
championship collects $100,000 in prize
money.

Chapter 5
Junior Drag Racing

In November, 1992, the National Hot Rod Association started the Junior Drag Racing League for young drivers between ages 8 and 17. There are now about 40 drag strips in the United States that allow junior racing.

Junior dragsters are half-sized copies of Top Fuelers, funny cars, or pro stocks. Their engines are only five horsepower. Racing on an one-eighth mile (201.1-meter) strip, they record times of about 13 seconds. Top speeds

Young drivers stand beside their cars on the junior drag racing circuit.

record times of about 13 seconds. Top speeds are about 50 miles (80.5 kilometers) per hour.

Most junior dragsters are made from kits. About 80 different companies make the kits. Building and racing your own dragster is a fun way to get involved in this amazing sport. Who knows? You may someday be setting new speed records in a Top Fueler of your own!

Glossary

amateur–someone who competes in a sport but who is not paid

blowover–describes a dragster that leaves the ground and tilts straight upward

burnout area–the area of the dragstrip where the drivers spin their tires to clean them

cancer–a very serious and often deadly disease which spreads throughout the body

chief wrench–leader of a pit crew; chief mechanic

Christmas tree–name for a set of colored lights used to start drag races

clutch–the part of the car used to connect and disconnect the engine to the transmission

disqualify–to be prevented from competition because of a violation of the rules

drag meet–a day or weekend of drag racing

dragster–a drag-racing car

drag strip–a paved, quarter-mile (.4 kilometer), straight surface used for drag racing

elapsed time–the time it takes to travel from the starting line to the finish line

eliminate–to remove by defeating in a contest

e. t.–short for elapsed time

heat–one run down a drag strip

horsepower–a unit of measure used to indicate the power of an engine

muscle car–cars which have been rebuilt and made more powerful

nitro–short for an explosive mixture of nitromethane and alcohol that is used as fuel in Top Fuelers and funny cars

pit crew–the mechanics who work on a driver's car

pre-stage light–the small amber light at the top of the Christmas Tree. When lit, it tells the driver to move toward the starting line.

rail–another name for Top Fuel cars

rev–to accelerate

shutdown strip–the strip at the end of a drag strip, used by drivers for slowing down

slingshot–another name for a Top Fuel car

speed trap–the part of the drag strip where electronic beams measure a car's speed

stage light–the second small amber light on the Christmas Tree. It goes on when the dragster is on the starting line.

stiletto–another name for Top Fuel cars

supercharger–a device for increasing the power of an internal combustion engine by changing the mixture of fuel and air

Top Fuel–a class of dragster with a supercharged, nitromethane burning, fuel-injected aluminum engine

top eliminator–the winning dragster that has eliminated all competition

wrench–a mechanic

To Learn More

Cockerham, Paul W. *Drag Racing*. Race Car
Legends. Philadelphia: Chelsea House, 1997.

Hintz, Martin. *Top Fuel Drag Racing*. Drag
Racing. Mankato, Minn.: Capstone
Press, 1996.

McKenna, A. T. *Drag Racing*. Fast Tracks. Edina,
Minn.: Abdo & Daughters, 1998.

Pitt, Matthew. *Drag Racer*. Built for Speed. New
York: Children's Press, 2001.

Some Useful Addresses

Don Garlits Museum of Drag Racing
13700 Southwest 16th Avenue
Ocala, Florida 34473

This museum features a large race car collection, including *Swamp Rat I*. This is one of "Big Daddy" Garlits's most famous dragsters.

National Hot Rod Association (NHRA)
2035 Financial Way
Glendora, CA 91741

The National Hot Rod Association sponsors the Junior Drag racing League. Membership in the Junior Drag Racing League includes a subscription to the newspaper *Jr. Dragster*. Write to the NHRA address for more information.

Index